The Great Famine: The History of t]
19th (

By Charles River Editors

An illustration depicting the famine

About Charles River Editors

Charles River Editors provides superior editing and original writing services across the digital publishing industry, with the expertise to create digital content for publishers across a vast range of subject matter. In addition to providing original digital content for third party publishers, we also republish civilization's greatest literary works, bringing them to new generations of readers via ebooks.

Sign up here to receive updates about free books as we publish them, and visit Our Kindle Author Page to browse today's free promotions and our most recently published Kindle titles.

Introduction

An illustration depicting Irish emigration

The Irish Potato Famine

"I have called it an artificial famine: that is to say, it was a famine which desolated a rich and fertile island that produced every year abundance and superabundance to sustain all her people and many more. The English, indeed, call the famine a 'dispensation of Providence;' and ascribe it entirely to the blight on potatoes. But potatoes failed in like manner all over Europe; yet there was no famine save in Ireland." – John Mitchel, Young Ireland Movement

Anyone who has ever heard of "the luck of the Irish" knows that it is not something to wish on someone, for few people in the British Isles have ever suffered as the Irish have. As one commissioner looking into the situation in Ireland wrote in February 1845, "It would be impossible adequately to describe the privations which they habitually and silently endure...in many districts their only food is the potato, their only beverage water...their cabins are seldom a protection against the weather...a bed or a blanket is a rare luxury...and nearly in all their pig and a manure heap constitute their only property." Even his fellow commissioners agreed and expressed "our strong sense of the patient endurance which the laboring classes have exhibited under sufferings greater, we believe, than the people of any other country in Europe have to sustain."

Still, in their long history of suffering, nothing was ever so terrible as what the Irish endured during the Great Potato Famine that struck the country in the 1840s and produced massive upheaval for several years. While countless numbers of Irish starved, the famine also compelled many to leave, and all the while, the British were exporting enough food from Ireland on a daily basis to prevent the starvation. Over the course of 10 years, the population of Ireland decreased by about 1.5 million people, and taken together, these facts have led to charges as severe as genocide. At the least, it indicated a British desire to remake Ireland in a new mold. As historian Christine Kinealy noted, "As the Famine progressed, it became apparent that the government was using its information not merely to help it formulate its relief policies, but also as an opportunity to facilitate various long-desired changes within Ireland. These included population control and the consolidation of property through various means, including emigration... Despite the overwhelming evidence of prolonged distress caused by successive years of potato blight, the underlying philosophy of the relief efforts was that they should be kept to a minimalist level; in fact they actually decreased as the Famine progressed."

Although the Famine obviously weakened Ireland and its people, it also stiffened Irish resolve and helped propel independence movements in its wake. By the time the Famine was over, it had changed the face of not just Ireland but also Great Britain, and it had even made its effects felt across the Atlantic in the still young United States of America.

The Great Famine: The History of the Irish Potato Famine during the Mid-19th Century looks at the history of the notorious famine and its results. Along with pictures and a bibliography, you will learn about the Irish Potato Famine like never before, in no time at all.

The Great Famine: The History of the Irish Potato Famine during the Mid-19th Century
About Charles River Editors
Introduction
   Chapter 1: Political Background
   Chapter 2: The Potato Blight
   Chapter 3: The Export of Food
   Chapter 4: The Effects of the Famine
   Chapter 5: Responses to the Famine
   Chapter 6: The Consequences of the Famine
   Online Resources
   Bibliography

Chapter 1: Political Background

The island of Ireland was conquered by the English Crown in the early medieval period, but much of the island was beyond the control of the English Royal Governments and the majority of Ireland was independent by 1500. Beginning with Henry VIII of the Tudor Dynasty, who claimed to be the monarch of Ireland, the English fought a series of wars to make good their claims.[1] By 1603, the English monarchy effectively controlled the island and introduced widespread political, social and religious changes. In particular, they encouraged the English and other settlers to emigrate to Ireland, where they were given land, as with the "Plantation of Ulster." These settlers soon became the economic and political elite in the country.

By the late 1600s, these colonists and their descendants largely owned most of the land in Ireland. After a series of rebellions and confiscations, the old Irish elite were dispossessed, and many were exiled. The native Gaelic-speaking population was largely Catholic, in contrast to the settlers who were overwhelmingly Protestant. Ireland was dominated by a small number of Protestant landowners, who had established a series of Penal Laws, discriminating against Catholics in order to preserve their position at the apex of Irish society and their privileged status. Despite the repeal of the Penal Laws in the eighteenth century, the Anglo-Irish elite continued to dominate Ireland, economically, socially, and politically, well into the nineteenth century.

Politically, Ireland was part of the United Kingdom after the 1801 Act of Union. This led to the union of the British and Irish parliaments. The Irish parliament was dominated by the Anglo-Irish Protestant elite, who excluded Catholics from political office. With the Act of Union, Irish MPs could sit in the British Parliament. Despite the Act of Union, the country was still dominated by the Anglo-Irish elite, who were only a small minority in an overwhelmingly Catholic country.[2] By the 1840s, Catholics had won some political rights, such as the right to hold political office. However, in general, the Catholic majority were very much second class citizens, and were economically and politically subordinated to the Anglo-Irish elite.

Famine was not new to Ireland. Every few years there was a partial failure of the potato crop or some natural disaster that resulted in a famine. In the 1740s, an unseasonable frost destroyed the crops in the fields,[3] which led to widespread hunger and epidemics and by the end of the famine, and some 10% of the population died over a two-year period. There were also small and localized food crises in Ireland in the 1820s and the 1830s. However, the famine in the period of1845-1850 was to be an unprecedented one that changed Irish history.

---

[1] The English conquest was driven by the fear that Ireland would be used as a base to attack England by Catholic Spain and to secure new lands for its population.

[2] Irish MPs sat in the Westminster Parliament and they had little or no effect on policy. Real power lay with the British administration in Dublin Castle. [2] Ó Gráda, Cormac (1993), *Ireland before and after the Famine: Explorations in Economic History 1800–1925*, Manchester University Press

[3] It is estimated that one in ten people died in this famine, caused by unusually cold weather. Ibid.

During the Napoleonic Wars, there was a dramatic expansion in tillage in Ireland. This long conflict created a demand for food from Britain to feed its navy and army, which required a large agricultural workforce. Furthermore, many landowners decided to grow crops on their lands which meant there was less land for small tenant farmers. Rents rose, and it was increasingly difficult for Irish cottiers and labourers to obtain sufficient land to meet a family's needs. The ability to rent a piece of land could often mean the difference between starvation and survival for many Irish Catholics. Because of the changing rural economy, more and more people came to rely on the potato. This was chiefly because potatoes could grow quickly, and did not require much land to provide a large crop.[4]

The root vegetable was introduced into Ireland in the seventeenth century by Walter Raleigh, and the population had grown dependent upon it since then. During the eighteenth century, the potato was very important in the Irish diet, and had come to be a staple in the Irish diet by 1800 for up to one-third of the population.

At first, it was treated as an addition to the diet, consumed with milk, fish, and bread. However, as Irish society became poorer and the farms became smaller, more and more people were forced to depend upon the potato for food, consumed boiled or in the form of potato cakes. The Irish consumed large amounts of potatoes, especially the poor. The diet of the Irish peasants, although monotonous, provided them with all the nutrition they needed. Potatoes are a very nutritious food, and Irish society and economy was almost wholly dependent on a single crop. It facilitated the development of the cottier system, where a cheap, agricultural workforce could work the land of the Anglo-Irish elite, who grew increasingly rich, using the cheap, Irish workforce to produce cheap food for England, which rapidly industrializing at the time. The Irish peasant was reliant upon only one variety of the crop, namely the 'Irish Lumper' potato, which was highly nutritious and resistant to indigenous diseases.

Irish society was shaped by the system of landownership. Land was the main source of wealth in the country prior to the Famine, and continued to be so after it ended. The land was largely rented by Protestant landlords to Catholic tenants. Their holdings were often very small--it was not unusual for tenant farmers to have only two or three acres of land. One in four Irish tenants had farms that were only 1.5-2 hectares in size. This group and their families made up the majority of the population. By some measurements, over one-half of the nation consisted of subsistence farmers, and any chance event could reduce a tenant farmer and his family to penury and starvation.

Another issue in Ireland was that often, when a tenant died, they divided their lands among all their children, which is an age-old Gaelic tradition. However, this practice of sub-division meant that, over time, the holdings of the Irish cottiers were reduced further in size each generation. There was not enough land for them to produce anything else than potatoes. This meant that they

---

[4] Ibid

could not produce food for the market and their farms were used simply to provide for their food supply for the year--if they were lucky. Such was the hunger for land that, more and more, marginal land came into use, such as in hilly and upland areas. At this time, many of the islands off the west coast, such as the Arran Islands, became densely populated, as people desperately sought land. Before the famine, an official British government report indicated that poverty was endemic, and that some one-third of all Irish small farmers could not support their families after paying their rent. The majority of the poor lived in one- or two-roomed cabins. Despite this and other reports, there was nothing done to change the situation, and the Irish poor continued to live in the shadow of famine and in wretched poverty.[5] Visitors to Ireland remarked that poverty was universal in rural districts such as Skibberrean. In County Cork, especially in the hill areas, one journalist witnessed the 'the most dreadful privations' in the early 1840s, even before the Famine.[6]

There was a large labouring class who were often landless and who would often wander the country looking for work, especially at harvest time. Up to one-quarter of the population would migrate to England and Scotland during harvest time, and there they would earn wages which often helped them and their families avoid starvation in the winter. Many labourers often relied on what they could grow in a small garden, or acre of land, in order to survive during the periods when they were not working on the landlord's own land and other farms in order to pay their rent.

Many Irish peasants lived in a form of feudal dependency on their landlords, in a barter economy. Any cash money they earned would usually be given to their landlords to pay their rents. They would swap their surplus of potatoes, if they had any, to purchase necessities, such as utensils, in the local markets. Many Irish families were self-sufficient, often making everything that they needed. The main fuel of the Irish was peat, dug from the many bogs on the island.

There was also a very large class of desperately poor people who wandered the country, begging. The towns and the cities were large and growing, but by and large, Ireland was an agrarian society. There was some industry in the urban centers. Limerick was called 'a second Liverpool' by William Makepeace Thackeray because of its industries. By and large, Ireland was not industrializing like England and Scotland prior to the Great Hunger, and this meant that the surplus population in the countryside could move to the towns and cities for work. Poverty was not just confined to rural Ireland. In urban centers there was widespread poverty, even by the standards of the time. In Dublin and elsewhere, the poverty was deemed greater than in Indian cities. There were many successful merchants, and agents for landlords who composed the middle class, but this class was relatively small.

---

[5] *Foster, R.F (1988), Modern Ireland 1600–1972, Penguin Group*

[6] ibid

Irish society was very unfair, and marked by great poverty. The majority of the people lived on the verge of disaster, which led to a great deal of agrarian unrest. There were many secret societies in the country, such as the 'Ribbon Men,' who violently attacked the landlords and their agents. Murder, intimidation, and arson were very common in rural Ireland, as secret societies sought to secure better terms for the poor tenants.[7] Ireland was a very violent society to the point where many in the British government believed the island to be on the verge of outright rebellion in the years prior to the Famine.[8]

Another problem was that the Irish population expanded rapidly in the eighteenth century. The Catholic communities grew at a much faster rate than the Protestants. By 1800, the population on the island of Ireland was some 6 million. By 1840, it was well over 8 million and the country was one of the most densely populated in Europe. The reasons behind the population increase are varied. It seems the Irish poor tended to marry earlier, and the availability of the potato allowed an increasingly impoverished society to expand and grow. The potato was a cheap and nutritious form of food and it allowed people, despite their poverty, to survive longer, and many of the poor were surprisingly healthy. This, in turn, allowed the Irish poor to have large families. Ireland's population growth meant there were more and more people who were, at the same time, becoming increasingly impoverished. In contrast to many other countries in Europe at the time, Irish society was only becoming poorer.[9]

The expansion of the population was not linear, and there were many demographic crises before the famine. Ireland suffered harvest failures and epidemics of diseases such as cholera and typhus, which resulted in many deaths. However, because of the cheapness and availability of potatoes, the population was quick to recover and continued to expand rapidly, especially when the harvest was good.[10] According to some historians, it appears that Ireland before the Famine was on the brink of economic and social disaster. However, there is another school of thought that argues that this was not the case. Ireland before the Famine had a complex socio-economic system which allowed the population to grow and remain relatively healthy, despite the observations of some who believed there was a want of 'improvement' among the farmers.[11] The argument goes that, but for an unforeseen event, Ireland was not doomed to experience terrible famine.

---

[7] There were many different agrarian secret societies in Ireland, all seeking to improve the conditions of the Irish tenants. See Duffy, Peter (2007), The Killing of Major Denis Mahon, HarperCollins.

[8] Boyce G., *'Nineteenth Century Ireland,'* (Gill and Macmillan 2005).

[9] The Skibbereen Famine Commemoration Committee. Sources for the history of the Great Famine in Skibbereen and surrounding area, vol II, p. 4.

[10] Mokyr, Joel (1983), Why Ireland starved, A quantitative and analytical history of the Irish economy 1800–1850. Manchester University Press: Manchester.

[11] The Times, November 28th 1845.

Chapter 2: The Potato Blight

The first reports of blight, which was totally unknown in Ireland or Europe, came in 1844. Experts believe that the blight was imported into Europe from Latin America, where it was endemic. Potato crops had been decimated in the past, but the blight was something new. Not only did it have an impact on the potato crop in Ireland, but throughout Europe as well. The blight attacked the potato, because it had no resistance to the disease. In August 1845, the Prime Minister of Great Britain, Sir Robert Peel, was informed that the "potato blight" that had been a problem in America had made its way to Southern England, but while the United States was able to grow enough different crops to offset the potato blight, it was a far greater inconvenience in England. Much worse, he was warned, would be the effect it would have on the people of Ireland, who depended on the potato much like those in Asian countries depended on rice.

Peel

October 1845 brought more bad news, as the poorest among the Irish began digging the potatoes that would have to feed them through the winter. That is when they discovered the true extent of the blight and reached out to the British Parliament for help. To his credit, Peel tried to move quickly to avoid disaster. In 1847, the *Dublin University Magazine* noted, "In the autumn of 1845, it was discovered that a disease had attacked the potato in Ireland, and in several other parts of the world. Of the actual existence of such a disease there was no doubt…Some of the journals in Ireland, supposed most to represent the aristocracy, persisted in vigorously denying the existence of any failure to more than a very partial extent…To profess belief in the existence of a formidable potato blight, was as sure a method of being branded a radical, as to propose to destroy the Church. Sir Robert Peel was then at the head of affairs, and the ministry certainly foresaw the coming calamity. Inquiries were made as to the substance that would be the best and cheapest substitute for the potato. Indian corn was adopted, and without any public excitement on the subject, orders were given by the government for the importation of Indian corn to the amount of L100,000. This timely precaution, and the subsequent judicious distribution of this store, had the effect of bringing the people through the winter of 1845, without exposing them to any sever privations…"

While importing corn solved some of Ireland's problems, it caused a hue and cry among much of the rest of Great Britain because it drove down the price English farmers could expect to get for their grain crops. As a result, Peel was unable to keep the help coming, even though he put his own position on the line. The magazine article continued, "It was, however, the misfortune of famine-stricken Ireland, and a deep misfortune almost all men in Ireland now feel it to be, that party combinations (we say not now, how justifiable or honorable) removed from office the man who had shown himself alone, perhaps, of living statesmen, alive to the exigencies of the crisis, and capable of boldly and efficiently meeting them. It was an occasion upon which no statesman could efficiently serve the country out of office…and with the removal of Peel from office he lost the power of even assisting to obviate the danger, which, we do believe, had he remained in office, he would successfully have met."

By the late Autumn of 1845, it was reported that in some areas, up to one-third of the potato crop had been lost[12] (it should be remembered that there was not a total failure of the potato crop, even during the worse year of the Famine in 1847), and unfortunately, the destruction of much of the potato crop in the country continued each year from 1845-1850. At first it was hoped the impact of this new disease would be limited. However, there was no way of treating the infected crop, and the fact that all Irish potatoes were Lumpers, which had no natural resistance to the disease, meant that the blight was particularly devastating. Even though some believed the reports were exaggerated, there was soon near panic in the elite.

---

[12] The potato blight originated in Latin America, however, local potatoes were largely immune to the fungus. Because the variety of potatoes used in Ireland had no resistance, they were devastated.

A contemporary depiction of an Irish woman and her two kids

The blight was a novelty to many of the Irish peasants. Potato diseases were not unknown as they had caused partial failures in recent decades, but the blight was beyond the experience of Irish farmers. They were amazed to find their potatoes blackened and inedible when they were dug from the ground. Because of the great poverty of the poorest elements of society, many tenant farmers simply did not have any food reserves. Typically, when the harvest was gathered, people began to eat the potato immediately, as the supplies from the last harvest had already been eaten. Upon discovering the potato crop was ruined, many knew they would ultimately starve. A large number of tenant farmers and laborers did not have the financial surplus to help them over the crisis. The economy of many poorer areas of the country was based on a barter system, and little money actually circulated in these areas, which meant they could not purchase the available food. Those that did have some money were forced to make the decision whether to pay their rent to the landlord or buy food.

The potato blight was a disaster for many families, as when the potatoes failed, they did not have enough to eat and they and their families were at risk of losing their land and livelihood. Many people immediately sought relief from the local community where it was traditional to help those who were in distress, especially those who were family members and neighbours. At first, the Irish poor shared their resources, and this helped many through the hard winter of 1854-1846. People soon began to hoard supplies, when they started to run out of food. This meant that traditional support networks which had helped people in previous famines had collapsed, and many more began to starve. People bemoaned the fact that traditional charity and neighbourliness had ended, and people had begun to turn on each other, like 'wolves.'[13] Some people became so desperate for food they made the fateful decision to eat their seed potatoes, needed to plant the next season's potato harvest. This meant they would not have a potato harvest the following season and they'd condemned themselves to starvation. Within months of the blight's first appearance, it was clear that the situation for many of Ireland's poor was disastrous.[14] At this time, it became common for families to eat grass and nettles. Boiled nettles, eaten as a broth, was a frequent meal.

One of the most pressing problems was that people continued to hear that they were going to receive more corn, yet they never saw it coming. In the middle of March 1846, the *Cork Reporter* decried the "evils of delay" and wrote that "while parties in the state and elsewhere are squabbling among themselves as to what is to be deemed the starvation test, sickness and famine are already doing their work. The afflicting spectacle of man and wife borne to the grave from fever was witnessed in our streets yesterday. The melancholy procession and the cry by which they were followed, sufficiently attested the class to which they belonged -- they were of the poor. Three of their orphans are struggling with the same malady and remain in the same building from which they were removed. How many, let us ask, must perish before any of the four bills latterly passed is in operation, or any of the food in hand distributed? Are we to have nothing and hear of nothing but precautions? Will the Fabian policy conquer hunger and subdue in pestilence? As yet no family has had a meal of the state-imported corn. It is here -- it is on the way -- it is grinding -- sailing -- travelling from one estuary to another. It is talked of -- one day it is off the harbor, another at the quays; the next it is reloaded and wafted won the river, and the last announcement left it off the coast of Dingle, where the ship that bore it loomed through the mist like the Flying Dutchman, disappearing, perhaps, to attract the anxious gaze of the watchers on some other shore. We have the substantial proof of food being really here in the daily marching and counter-marching of marines and regulars, but beyond that we have no gratification."

---

[13] There were increasingly reports of people taking from poorer neighbors, which would have been unthinkable prior to the Famine. This was perhaps an indication of the societal breakdown caused by Famine conditions. The Limerick Reporter, Tuesday November 30, 1847.

[14] Royal Commission into the Condition of the Poorer Classes in Ireland [35], H.C. 1836 xxx, 35.

People were so desperate for something to eat that they continued to eat the obviously tainted corn, which naturally spread sickness around the countryside. The *Cork Reporter* article explained, "The people do not well know how to apply or where to come to; the distant parishes have heard rumors, but yet require information. They have received hints and read letters once or twice, but there is no public proclamation of the terms on which they are to apply for sustenance. They have gone on eating or fasting on the tainted potato, imbibing mortal disease, and have sickened, died or starved, while the machinery of grand jury and other intervention was preparing. Food and employment ought to be afforded at once, instantly. We have said so over and over; we repeated the warning until we grew tired of the reiteration. … Unsound potatoes have bred typhus. The sick are in some cases quintupled; contagion is fearful; even the word we fear to write -- cholera is apprehended. Why is this? Where is it to end? Precautions were taken. Every wise and sufficient antidote was contemplated. The plans were faultless, the scheme of the campaign against the double foe of famine and pestilence was without a flaw. Sir R. Peel assures us he had foreseen all that was to happen, but how many are they who have gone to the grave through the wards of the hospitals while he and his colleagues were quarreling and pondering, resigning and resuming office? We repeat our question: what is the number of dead we must first count over before food will begin to be distributed?"

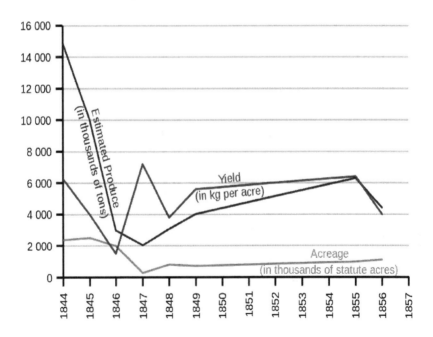

A graph showing the drop in potato production after 1844

While the politicians haggled about who was going to do what for whom, journalists continued to warn about the dangers facing Irish farmers, most of whom had lost as much as half their food supply. Peel's primary opponent, Lord Russell, was a firm believer in laissez-faire economics, and he was even quoted as claiming "the judgement of God sent the calamity to teach the Irish a lesson." Many agreed with him, including James Wilson, who wrote in *The Economist*, "It is no man's business to provide for another. ... If left to the natural law of distribution, those who deserve more would obtain it." However, with the law of supply and demand governing potato sales, the poor were slowly being winnowed out. The *Cork Reporter* noted in early March 1846, "But on the part of the poor, the struggle will be severe. Even at present, the price is beyond their reach; but this is in a great measure owing to the habit of forestalling. The potatoes are purchased before they enter the market, and there retailed to the consumer at an enormous profit. Thus while they bring in the market from 9d to 11d per weight, they are selling from the boats at 7 d. . . . During the week a gentleman, observing four cartloads of fine-looking potatoes in the street, asked the owner the price. The answer was, 'Sir, we couldn't sell them under sixpence;' yet though offered at those terms, they had been brought from within a mile of Mallow. The consumer, however, was probably nothing better for the moderation of the owner, for we dare say they fell into the hands of the forestaller, and were by him sold at nearly double the sixpence. We mention these facts, as it is well that, while we take all prudent precautions to meet any danger of which there may be reasonable apprehension, people should be warned against lending themselves to either pecuniary or political designs by exciting fears and spreading alarms for which there is no foundation."

Russell

In March 1846, Sir Peel was able to get the Labor Rate Act to Ireland passed through the British Parliament, authorizing Irish officials to tax local districts and thus raise money to hire needy people to do public works. The Act granted further money as aid to those areas that were so destitute that no money could be raised. As one man writing in April 1847 explained, "The provisions of the Labor Rate Act were simple enough. In every barony which the Lord Lieutenant proclaimed in a state of distress, extraordinary presentment sessions were to be held, at which the magistrates and cess-payers were to have the power of presenting for public works to an indefinite extent, subject only to the control of the Board of Works. The sums so presented were to be at once advanced by the Treasury, to be replaced by instalments that would spread the repayment of the entire, with interest, over a period varying at the discretion of the Treasury, from four to twenty years…In addition to the enormous expenditure under the Labor Rate Act, it must be remembered that, in many districts, the landed proprietors undertook to employ all the poor independently of any such provision; that, in others, the provisions of the summary Drainage Act were made available for the same purpose, and that sums that never or can be calculated distributed as gratuitous relief -- sums ostensibly given which appeared in no list of charity subscriptions, which yet form by far the largest proportion of what has been so given; and remembering all this, some estimate may be formed of what has been done by the holders of property in Ireland for the suffering poor…"

Unfortunately, while the plan sounded good on paper, it contained several serious flaws. The first was that the work given was forbidden by law from being profitable. For example, this meant the laborers could not build railroads because there were no new ones authorized to run in Ireland, and they could not seed meadows because that might give the Irish husbandman an advantage over his English counterpart. Thus, the hired workers could only build roads and bridges that were neither needed nor wanted. The writer addressed this when he wrote, "We believe and trust that the demoralizing effect of this upon the habits of the Irish laborer have been overrated; partly, perhaps, because the Irish laborer had few lessons or habits of patient industry to unlearn. What we regret is, the lost opportunity of inculcating better habits. Had these laborers been taught to feel that they were employed upon that which it was of real importance should be done-- had they been employed, under active discipline and careful superintendence, in the formation of the earthwork of railway, or engaged in the reclamation of some waste land, how well might they have been taught the lesson, that the remuneration of labor must, in the long run, depend, in a great degree, upon its productiveness. The employment given under the Labor Rate Act had a double fault; the wages were too low, and the work too light; it taught the people neither side of the lesson which employers and laborers in Ireland equally need to learn – 'a good day's wages for a good day's work.'"

Another flaw was that the people hired were too weak to do manual labor. The author castigated the Parliament for creating this situation: "It is difficult to trace this history without indignation. We can understand the verdict of the coroner's jury, who in days, when inquest were held in Ireland upon the bodies of the men found dead upon the highway, returned upon the body of a man who died in starvation while toiling at the public works, and fell dead of exhaustion with the implements of labor in his hand, a verdict of murder against the ministers who had neglected the first responsibility of government. Can we wonder if the Irish people believe -- and believe it they do -- that the lives of those who have perished, and who will perish, have been sacrificed by a deliberate compact to the gains of English merchants, and if this belief has created among all classes a feeling of deep dissatisfaction, not only with the ministry but with English rule…"

The final and most damning flaw was that the Act contained a clause saying that the government would in no way intervene in the food supply. The author of the 1847 article saved his most virulent criticism for that: "The introduction of the Labor Rate Act was coupled by a declaration on the part of the premier, which appeared almost to amount to a pledge, that with the supply of food to the country government did not intend to interfere; that this should be left entirely to the ordinary resources of commercial enterprise; and that government were resolved in no manner to interfere with the ordinary operations of the speculators or traffickers in human food…Tell us not that it was beyond the power of the combinations, which the strength of the British Empire could have wielded, to have brought to the ports of Ireland subsistence for all her people…The opportunity was lost; and Britain is now branded as the only civilized nation which would permit her subjects to perish of famine, without making a national effort to supply them with food..."

As more people died, more became desperate. As if the hunger wasn't bad enough, people had to watch neighbors dropping dead and wondering who would be next, including possibly themselves or a family member. Naturally, people continued to rail against the increasing prices and scarcity of grain. The *Cork Reporter* reported in an article entitled "Further Rise in the Prices of Grain," "Notwithstanding the unprecedented arrivals of grain into the port of Dublin, prices still continue to advance. At the Corn Exchange today considerable excitement prevailed and wheat, according to official market note, went up 1 shilling 6 pence…As before remarked, the supplies are pouring in from all quarters; the river is filled with shipping, containing cargoes of flour and other breadstuffs, and the greatest inconvenience is felt from the want of sufficient storage to remedy which temporary sheds have been erected along the north wall at the Customhouse; but even with this makeshift the accommodation is extremely defective. It is the opinion of some of the leading factors here that there will be no material (if any) reduction in the price of bread for two months to come; but that about the middle of March the foreign arrivals must tell, and that speculators may as well be prepared in time for a tremendous reaction."

The second blight on the potatoes created a downward spiral of crop failure and hunger because, unlike most vegetables, potatoes are not grown from seeds but from other healthy potatoes that are stored away through the winter to be planted the following spring. Thus, the blight didn't just kill the crop it attacked but also damaged future crops, especially since the "seed potatoes" might still carry the contagion. Making matters worse, many farmers who were desperate for something to eat exacerbated things by trying to plant the potatoes too early in the season.

On top of that, other crops were also suffering during this period, including the all-important wheat. *Derry Journal* reported on this on February 6, 1847: "The wheat crop at one time showed signs of recovering that unhealthfulness which we noticed in our last report; but we regret to say that latterly it has retrograded in most fields, which the excessive rains only can account for. The plants are generally thin on the ground, and their appearance anything but vigorous; but a good spring may yet bring this crop into a promising condition. Owing to the favorable weather at the commencement of the month, a considerable breadth of ground was put down with spring sown wheat; and we should think that by this time there is a full average of that grain committed to the soil."

While 1847 was the worst year and would be forever known as Black '47, the famine hung on for several more years. For instance, in March 1849, one author observed, "A renewed and extensive failure of the potato crop has added greatly to the sufferings of the poor, and increased the perplexities which have involved all other classes of society. The burden of poor rates has become intolerable to a people who have been themselves the principal sufferers from the loss of their crops; and the prospect of the aggravation of the pressure during the ensuing year from the continued and increasing distress and destitution in the country, has paralyzed the energies of even the most sanguine and the most resolute. The peculiar evils of the present system of poor laws in Ireland, and their great inaptitude for such a country, has also naturally tended to check all exertion to prevent an increase of the rates, as the most active and well-disposed proprietor finds that all the employment he can give to his poor is of little avail without an extensive cooperation among his neighbors, which it is, from various causes, impracticable to attain, while the ill effects of a system by which such vast numbers are fed upon public doles have, it is too plain, only increased their indolence and indisposition to earn their bread by manly exertion. This system, continued in one shape or other since the Labor Rate Act was passed, while it is fast swallowing up all private property, has at the same time, produced incalculable evils, in rendering the mass of the population listless and dead to every feeling of independence, an effect peculiarly disastrous to the case of the Irish peasantry. Altogether the prospects of the country are most gloomy, the very opposite to those which a well-ordered state should exhibit."

Chapter 3: The Export of Food

Though it may be hard to believe, historical research has shown that Ireland was a net exporter of food during the Great Famine from 1845-1850. This was true even during the height of the Famine, and many merchants and landlords earned vast sums from the export of foodstuffs. According to historians of the period, it was only the potato that failed during the Famine, while other crops remained unaffected. In the livestock industry, cows, pigs, and chickens were being fed so that they could be exported. While Ireland's livestock was being well feed and fattened, children were dying on the streets and in the fields. Wheat, beans, barley, and other crops were plentiful and yielded a good harvest. It has been estimated that even though many died due to starvation, the country was producing enough food to feed many of those in great need.

In 1847, the year regarded as the height of the Famine, the country had a record year for food exports, including bacon, calves, butter, and cereals. Even the areas hardest hit by the Famine were exporting food to Britain and elsewhere, transported to ships under British military guard, to protect the food from being seized by the starving Irish.

During the Famine, food distribution was not the problem as it had been in other famines. The real problem in Ireland was not the lack of food, but the lack of funds and the poorest could not afford to buy enough food as a result.[15] Studies have shown that because of the shortage of potatoes and the increasing exports of Irish food, prices rose steeply from 1845-1849. This led to a situation that, even if the poor tenant farmers and the laborers had any money, that they could not have purchased an adequate amount of food with it. The real problem for Ireland, and why so many starved to death, was the fact that during the Famine the price of food was too high for the majority of the population. In a land of plenty, many died as a result.

The British government did provide some assistance for the poor who had no food, or who could not support themselves. However, the relief proved to be of little help, and even those it did help were left embittered by the form and nature of the help they received. Government relief efforts were organised by the local Poor Unions who, between 1845 and 1846, provided some food to the starving populace. Public works were provided as a form of assistance from 1845 to 1847, involving the poor working on roads and building harbors, but many of these projects were poorly planned and later acknowledged to be a waste of money by the British government, as many involved were building roads that led to nowhere. The work was hard for undernourished people to complete, and they were often ordered great distances to work on projects that were often far away. On one occasion, 300 people in County Galway were ordered to work on a road some 20 miles away from their homes. If they failed to carry out the work, they risked losing their relief. A starving crowd of men, women, and children walked to the new project, but many of them died during the walk.

With so many people now too weak to work, the public works projects were replaced by workhouses, where people could work indoors, and soup kitchens, which distributed food to those too weak to work. The *Cork Reporter* published the following resolutions passed in Dublin in early January 1846:

> "Resolved: That the workhouse being now fully occupied, there being no fewer

---

[15] Donnelly, James S., Jr. (1995), Poirteir, Cathal, ed., Mass Eviction and the Irish Famine: The Clearanc Revisited", from The Great Irish Famine, Dublin, Ireland: Mercier Press

than 499 inmates (the house being calculated for only 400), and great destitution prevailing in many parts of the union, the master be instructed, in any case in which a destitute person may present himself with a guardian's order for provisional admission, before sending such person away to give him a meal, consisting of a dinner's ration to be eaten in the house, and to charge same against the union at large.

"Resolved: That it is also expedient that a room should be procured in the differing districts within the union where destitution prevails; that such room be declared a poorhouse...for the purpose of affording additional relief under the present very extraordinary circumstances of the country. That the guardians make a list of the destitute in those districts, that that after due inquiry, provisional order be given entitling such persons a meal to be eaten in the room so declared a poor house, within each district. The meal to consist of a pint of soup or mill, and 1 1/2 lb. of brown bread for adults, and for children in proportion. That it be fully understood that this mode of relief is only intended to meet the present distressing emergency and that it shall cease with the emergency, or when there is accommodation in the house."

In the workhouses, the starving were obliged to work in return for food and clothing, and the work was often gruelling and hard. Families were separated in the workhouses, and males and females segregated. There were many instances of abuse in these institutions which were often overseen by brutal officials. Furthermore, the Workhouses were overcrowded, making them ideal breeding grounds for diseases such as typhus.[16] As well, the food was rarely adequate, and many went hungry in these institutions. Such was the reputation of the Workhouses that many of the Irish poor, despite their hunger, refused to enter them preferring to die in their simple cabins instead.

---

[16] The death rates in the Workhouse was very high. It was not uncommon for one in every ten inmates to die in 1847. Royal Commission into the Condition of the Poorer Classes in Ireland [35], H.C. 1848 xxx, 35.

Chapter 4: The Effects of the Famine

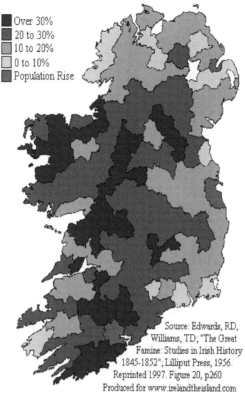

A map detailing the population drop in Ireland during the decade of the Famine

Ben Moore's graph indicating the population drop of Ireland and the contemporary population rise in the rest of Europe

The Famine devastated many areas of the country, but its effects were not felt evenly throughout the region. In addition, its impact on the classes and religions were also quite different. Religion was the great divide in Ireland. The country was polarized between the Protestants, who made up 22% of the population, and the Catholics, who made up the rest. Even so, the number of Catholics who died greatly exceeded the number of Protestants, which was the result of the great poverty of the Catholics, and in a famine, it is the poor who suffer the most. Because the poor were engaged in a monoculture, they were unable to secure enough food for themselves and their families. The rural poor, were made up of small tenant farmers and laborers, suffered the most due to their great dependence on the potato.

Beginning in 1845, the poor began to die in great numbers. The death rates rose sharply during the winter. The poor preferred to die in their homes, and it soon became a common occurrence for whole families to be found, dead, in their cabins. By 1846, the local graveyards could no longer cope with the numbers who were dying, and the Catholic Church was forced to consecrate new burial grounds for the many dying, which became known as Famine graveyards. Today, nearly every locality on the island of Ireland has one such 'Famine Graveyard.' The families of the poor, usually responsible for burying their loved ones, were too weak to bury them properly. As a result, the bodies of the dead were often left out in the open. The local authorities pressed unemployed men into service, or forced prisoners to collect these bodies and bury them.[17] The poor often abandoned their homes in the search of food, and many died in their forlorn attempts to find work or food, some of them by the side of the road. By the winter of 1845, large groups of poor people frequently wandered the roads and lanes of the country begging for food, but there was no food to spare.

The rural poor were not the only ones to suffer and die. The urban poor also suffered greatly, going hungry and dying in great numbers, especially among the unemployed and the laborers.[18] During the 'Great Hunger,' many tenant farmers could not pay their rent and were evicted by their landlords after falling into arrears. People were forcibly taken from their homes by landlords, and forced to become homeless wanderers, often with the support of police and the military. Landlords or their agents frequently forbade their tenants from helping those who were evicted. To ensure they did not return, many of the evictees' hovels and cabins were burned to the ground. Those evicted were often forced, not only to leave their homes, but their local areas as well. To be evicted during the Great Famine was almost a death sentence. Those who owned the least amount of land were most liable to be evicted. According to the Catholic Bishop of Meath, up to a quarter of those who were evicted had died within a year.[19]

The impact of the Famine varied from region to region. In 1845, the blight was felt hardest by those who lived in the poorest areas and on marginal lands, such as those in the upland areas. The blight decimated the food supply of the poorest of the poor, who were the least able to bear the loss of their precious potato crops. However, not all areas of the country experienced a disastrous potato harvest, and some farmers managed to retrieve at least a portion of the harvest. This is evident by the death rates from across the country in the period of 1845-1850. Some 24% of the population emigrated or died in Connacht, and 23% in the province of Munster. This compares to 12% in Ulster, and 16% in Leinster.[20]

Initially, the Famine was felt hardest in the West, and in part of Munster, reflecting the socio-economic structure of these regions. Areas such as Skibbereen in Country Cork became bywords for suffering In the winter of 1846 and early 1847, conditions in Skibberrean and the surrounding district deteriorated. In the townland of Drimelogue, 'one in four died that winter.'[21] The continuing lack of food prompted one Cork doctor to declare that 'not one in five will recover.' In these regions, the tenants' farms were generally small, and more poor and marginal land was in use. As a result, the local inhabitants were more likely to suffer from a disruption to their food supply. Some areas of the country, such as East Ulster, did not suffer much at first

---

[17] It was hard to get volunteers or even pay people to bury the dead because there was the fear of infection. Royal Commission into the Condition of the Poorer Classes in Ireland. [35], H.C. 1846 xxx, 35.

[18] The death rates in many southern towns and cities, such as Cork, were as high as in some rural regions. Killen, Richard (2003), A Short History of Modern Ireland, Gill and Macmillan Ltd.

[19] Mokyr, Joel (1983), Why Ireland starved, A quantitative and analytical history of the Irish economy 1800–1850

[20] Kennedy, Liam; Ell, Paul S; Crawford, E. M; Clarkson, L. A (1999), *Mapping The Great Irish Famine*, Four Courts Press

[21] Cork Examiner, December 10 1845. The Skibberreen Famine Commemoration Committee. Sources for the history of the Great Famine in Skibbereen and surrounding area, vol II, p. 4.

because it was more industrialized than the rest of Ireland. However, as the Famine persisted, and the blight continued to attack the potato crop, the areas that initially did not suffer greatly began to show real signs of distress, and mass hunger became evident.

By 1847 the Famine had spread to almost every area of the country. Even those areas in Leinster and Ulster that had been spared the worst of the disaster were now ravaged by famine. In 1847, the year the greatest number of people died, directly and indirectly from the Famine, is often referred to as "Black 1847." Urban areas, especially Dublin, saw a massive spike in the death rate, particularly in the vast slums. After 1847, some parts of the country began to recover, and many parts of Kerry and Cork for example, which had been the epicentre of the Famine, began to see signs of improvement in 1848. However, some areas of the country still saw mass starvation, such as in Limerick as late as 1850, which was the year that many historians believed the famine had ended.

Despite the uneven impact of the blight during the famine, the entire country suffered greatly. Potatoes made up a sizeable percentage of the nutritional intake of even relatively affluent people. Part of this hardship was because it led to a sharp rise in the price of all foodstuffs. As the supply of potatoes declined, they became more expensive, and people could afford to buy as much of this staple food. Other foodstuffs also became more expensive as people who could not afford potatoes tried to purchase other foods, such as barley and wheat, to make flour for bread. It is no wonder that the years coinciding with the Famine also saw a severe economic downturn. Because people spent all their money on food, they could no longer buy other essentials, such as clothes. This led to a dramatic contraction of the Irish economy, and mass unemployment and bankruptcies in the urban areas, even in the relatively affluent Belfast and Dublin. Though the effects of the Great Hunger differed from region to region, all of the country ultimately suffered as a result of the Famine.[22]

The Great Hunger, as it became known, killed many hundreds of thousands, but the greatest killer during the famine was not starvation. Instead, most people died of various diseases, which is typical of famines. Only a small percentage of those who died during the Great Famine did so due to lack of nutrition or starvation; people largely died as hunger had weakened their immune systems, creating environments where communicable diseases were easily spread.

The Famine also caused social breakdown as a result of the local infrastructure breaking down, especially due to local water supplies becoming polluted. Dysentery, caused by drinking infected water, was endemic in 1847, and killed. Typhus was another great killer. Even illnesses that usually were not serious killed people, because their immune systems were so severely weakened.

The main killers were fever, dysentery, cholera, smallpox, and pneumonia, the first two of

---

[22] The relief committee of Skibberrean to Sir R Routh, Sept 14 1846, p. 36.

which were the most lethal. Reliable estimates state that dysentery killed some 222,000 and 'fevers' killed 93,000. The government admitted the figures were incomplete and that the real number of deaths was probably considerably higher. In 1847, Dr. Dan Donovan of Skibberrean Cork estimated that between one-third and a half of the local population were laboring under fever and dysentery. Donovan contributed medical articles, especially on the effects of starvation and famine-related diseases to publications, such as the *Dublin Medical News,* and *The Lancet,* based upon the many autopsies he had undertaken during the height of the Famine. In his 'Observations on the Disease to which the Famine of last year gave Origin,' and on the morbid effects of Deficiency of Food,' he differentiated death due to starvation, and disease related to 'want of necessities.' In his obituary, it was noted that "observations of the post-mortem changes as a result of acute and chronic starvation, were so accurate and original as to establish him in the medical world as the chief authority regarding the distinction between death from famine and disease." Dr. Donovan also established that victims of famine often never fully recovered, as it was 'impossible to resurrect the energies of the truly famine struck.' These ideas influenced doctors around the world when treating the victims of famine, especially British doctors in India. The death rate spiked in the winter, as many of the starving people, had not the strength or the resources to provide themselves with proper clothing. This meant that many more died of illnesses, such as pneumonia. Another great killer at this time was food poisoning. Many people on the verge of starvation ate anything they could find, and many consumed food that was tainted or inedible, which killed in unknown numbers.[23] In particular, the practice of eating grass and nettles by desperate people, ultimately led to their deaths.

As noted above, many regions of Ireland were saved from the worst effects of mass starvation and distress, but they did not escape the disease. This was especially the case in many urban centers, such as Belfast. Those who did suffer during the Famine and/or those who were evicted from their land, often sought relief in urban centres. Desperate people wandered the roads of Ireland, weakened by hunger, and carrying diseases such as smallpox. When they made their way to urban centres such as Belfast, they brought the disease with them, resulting in many outbreaks of disease, such as dysentery and typhus. Countless died as a result, and not only the poor, but members of the middle class and the elite as well. Measures were measures taken to prevent the poor from coming into the towns and cities and spreading disease, but it proved impossible to stop them.

In the decade between 1845 and 1855, almost 3 million men, women and children left Ireland forever, bound for new homes in North America, Australia or other parts of Great Britain. The most fortunate were sent to these far off lands by their former landlords, who found it a better financial deal than continuing to rent small plots of land out. In fact, the years of the Irish Potato Famine saw many landlords shift from having many small-scale tenants renting their property to consolidating their land into large tracts that could support sheep or dairy farming.

---

[23] This is quite common in famines and food shortages, and is a significant killer. Ó Gráda, Cormac (2006), *Ireland's Great Famine: Interdisciplinary Perspectives*, Dublin Press

Through the years, this has led some to suspect that the English government deliberately caused the blight that led to the famine, and while this is unlikely, it is true that many a calloused politician observed that it ultimately solved the problem of overpopulation in Ireland. Charles Edward Trevelyan, the British Treasury Secretary for Ireland, wrote as far back as 1846 that with overpopulation "being altogether beyond the power of man, the cure has been applied by the direct stroke of an all-wise Providence in a manner as unexpected and as unthought of as it is likely to be effectual." In 1848, with an estimated million or more Irish already dead, he commented, "The matter is awfully serious, but we are in the hands of Providence, without a possibility of averting the catastrophe if it is to happen. We can only wait the result." Some months later, he asserted, "The great evil with which we have to contend is not the physical evil of the famine, but the moral evil of the selfish, perverse and turbulent character of the people." Likewise, in 1848, the English Chancellor of the Exchequer, wrote to a friend who owned an estate in Ireland: "I am not at all appalled by your tenantry going. That seems to be a necessary part of the process...We must not complain of what we really want to obtain."

Tragically, many Irishmen who left Ireland learned that they were no better off once they were on board the ships than they had been at home. Many unscrupulous men, attracted by the easy money to be had carrying large numbers of poor people to new homes, turned ships formerly used for shipping grain or cattle into passenger vessels. In doing so, however, they only made the most minimum changes possible, and many who boarded the ships, already weakened from years of starvation, did not live long enough to see their new homes. In fact, the ships were so notoriously bad that they earned the nickname "coffin ships." In August 1847, *The Toronto Globe* in Canada reported, "The *Virginius* from Liverpool, with 496 passengers, had lost 158 by death, nearly one third of the whole, and she had 180 sick; above one half of the whole will never see their home in the New World. A medical officer at the quarantine station on Grosse lie off Quebec reported that 'the few who were able to come on deck were ghastly, yellow-looking specters, unshaven and hollow-cheeked. . . not more than six or eight were really healthy and able to exert themselves. The crew of the ship were all ill, and seven had died. On the *Erin's Queen* 78 passengers had died and 104 were sick. On this ship the captain had to bribe the seamen with a sovereign for each body brought out from the hold. The dead sometimes had to be dragged out with boat hooks, since even their own relatives refused to touch them."

Although the Famine is associated with a great exodus out of Ireland, mass emigration was already underway before the Famine. Many thousands of Scots-Irish left Ulster for America in the eighteenth century.[24] In the 1830s, in the aftermath of the Napoleonic Wars, more and more Irish Catholics began to move abroad in order to search for a better life. It is believed that, from 1800 to 1850, some one million to one and a half million people left the country. The impact of the Famine was to greatly increase the number of those who were emigrating from the country. One authority estimates that some quarter of a million men, women, and children left the shores

---

[24] Fitzgerald and Lambkin, '*Migration in Irish History 1607-2007*', (Palgrave Macmillan 2008).

of Ireland. Some counties lost half of their population in the generation after the Great Hunger.

As part of the response to the Famine, many local relief committees believed that the only way to save people was by sending large numbers of people out of the country, through assisted emigration schemes. Relief committees around the country collected funds to charter ships to take large numbers of people out of the country. Many landlords helped pay the passage of their evicted tenants to new lands. Even though these schemes meant many people had to leave their ancestral homes, they undoubtedly saved many lives.[25]

Usually, emigration is confined to the young, and especially common among males. However, during the Famine, young and old alike left Ireland, and as many women as men. Entire extended families often emigrated, which meant they'd have to leave Ireland forever, never to return. Many simply left their small farms and cabins, selling everything they to purchase tickets for ships leaving Irish ports. Many emigrants relied on family members already abroad to pay for their fares, usually to join them or pre-existing Irish communities, especially in Britain. The destination of the emigrants was largely confined to the Britain, the United States, Canada, and Australia. These countries' economies were growing at this time, and they were in need of labour, and people to settle their vast territories. In general, the Irish were welcomed, however, over time tensions began to arise. The Irish were not welcome in many British cities as they were seen as driving down wages, and bringing diseases such as Typhus with them. Many thousands of Irish found their way to Canada, and there was massive immigration to cities such as Toronto. Soon many cities and towns in western Canada had significant Irish populations. This led to restrictions being imposed on Irish immigrants and led many more to seek a new life in the United States. However, the large Irish Catholic influx was not welcomed by all in America. and there were some tensions between the new immigrants and the resident population there as well.

The only way the emigrants could leave Ireland was by ship. Such was the desperation of people to leave the country, especially in 1847, they were willing to accept passage on any ship in the hope of fleeing hunger and disease. Many of the ships they took were not seaworthy. Many that left Irish ports sank in storms, and thousands died in shipwrecks. The ships soon had a terrible reputation and became known as Coffin Ships, due to the high number of deaths on board vessels that were often operated by unscrupulous Irish or British merchants and ship owners. It is estimated that some 100,000 Irish sailed on these Coffin Ships to Canada in 1847.[26] The conditions on the ships were so bad that up to one in five or more died on them. Many of those who died on-board were simply tossed overboard. These ships were ideal breeding grounds for disease. There was also a lack of food. Many who made it to their new homes died soon after disembarking. In Canada, in one notorious incident, some 5,000 people who were being held in Quarantine died after the passage across the Atlantic in a Coffin Ship.[27]

---

[25] Maxwell I., '*Everyday Life in 19th-Century Ireland*,' (The History Press Ireland 2012).

[26] Laxton, Edward (1997), *The Famine Ships: The Irish Exodus to America 1846–51*, Bloomsbury,

It has been estimated that during the years of the Great Famine, emigration from Ireland reached a record 250,000 in one year. According to a report released in 1851, "The emigration of the last three years gives an annual average of 268,469 persons, being not very short of the whole annual increase of the United Kingdom. If this emigration be analysed, the results as regards Ireland will be much more striking. For assuming nine-tenths of the emigration from Liverpool to be Irish (which is a low estimate), and even omitting altogether those who proceed from the Clyde, it will appear that the Irish emigration during the last three years has been 601,448; giving an average of 200,482 a year. Now the increase of population in Ireland between 1831 and 1841 as appears from the census return, was 407,723, in spite of an emigration amounting during the same years to 455,239, thus making the real increase to be 802,959, or 86,295 a year. Assuming the increase to have been at the same rate since 1841, when the population was returned at 8,175,238, it would give for the eight years to the close of 1849, 707,480 souls, or 88,435 per annum. At this rate, therefore, the population would be decreased in about in about eight years in about eight years by 1,000,000 souls by emigration alone; when it is also taken into account that the emigration comprises a large proportion of those who are in the vigour of life, and on whom the increase of our population chiefly depends, it may be assumed that its influence in checking such increase is even greater than the mere figures imply."

For many decades after the Famine, there continued to be large scale emigration from Ireland, which led to a decline in the Irish population. In 1840 there were eight and a half million people in Ireland, but in 1960, over a century later, there were only 4.5 million, despite the Irish having a high birth rate. Many Irish people had left the country for America or elsewhere prior to the Famine, and even more left because of the Famine.[28] Between 1856 and 1921, over four million Irish adults and children emigrated abroad.[29]

It has been estimated that from 1848 to 1870, 45,000 availed themselves of assisted migration to New South Wales, with over 3,000 of them being from Limerick.[30] Assisted migration schemes were usually well planned, and organized by the State, philanthropists, or estate owners.[31]

Female migration was on the increase, which may have affected marriage rates, which had decreased significantly in the post-famine years. This mass movement was to have dramatic consequences for the populations of many countries. Soon there were substantial Irish communities all over the world, helping to develop the economics in their new homes. However, since many of the Irish were Catholics, it led to sectarian tension with existing Protestant

---

[27] The exact numbers who died on these coffin ships may never be known, but it is believed to be in the many thousands. Fahey, D., "*A Fact Book of Irish History from the Earliest Times to 1969*" (Thorn island publishing.com 2012).

[28] 1885, Committal form L.D.A.

[29] Fitzgerald and Lambkin, '*Migration in Irish History 1607-2007*', (Palgrave Macmillan 2008) p 172.

[30] Chris O'Mahoney, 'Balancing the Sexes', *The Old Limerick Journal*, Vol. 23, Spring, Australian Edition, 1988.

[31] Duffy P., (2006) pp. 22-37.

communities in countries such as America and Canada.

Emigration remained a fact of life for many decades after the Famine; it even became somewhat of a tradition for younger family members to emigrate elsewhere in order to make a life for themselves, the vast majority never to return.

Emigration even continued even after Irish independence. This led to a continued fall in the population of Ireland. In 1960, there were only 4.5 million people in Ireland (The Republic and Northern Ireland), even with a high birth rate, even though in 1840 the Irish population was over eight million.

It was only in the 1960s that the population of the island stabilized and recovered, after over a century of decline in the aftermath of the Great Hunger.

A political cartoon from the 1880s with the caption: "In forty years I have lost, through the operation of no natural law, more than Three Million of my Sons and Daughters, and they, the Young and the Strong, leaving behind the Old and Infirm to weep and to die. Where is this to end?"

Chapter 5: Responses to the Famine

Ireland was a deeply religious society. People tended to explain events and phenomenon in religious terms. Many, both Catholic and Protestant, regarded the Famine as punishment for people's sins. Natural catastrophes were often seen as part of God's plan, a warning to people to mend their ways and live according to the teachings of the Church. Lord Trevelyan, a member of the Irish administration, publically stated that God was punishing the Irish with the Famine. Many of the Anglo-Irish elite, such as the landlords, believed the crisis to be the result of the Irish Catholics', feckless lifestyle, and their laziness. They pointed out that the Irish had too many children, and refused to improve their lot in life. This was typical of the time when issues such as economic trends were poorly understood and poverty was seen as self-inflicted. Despite thisr, the overwhelming response of Irish society, and indeed British society, was one of sympathy. Many, no matter their religion or background, regarded the event as a human tragedy, and they tried to help victims of the Famine if they were able.

The Famine drew an unprecedented response in Ireland and internationally, especially when it became apparent that it was not a typical food shortage, but a major famine. Relief Committees were established in nearly every locality. Usually formed by the local elite and members of the Protestant and Catholic gentry, they raised money for local people who suffered and experienced privation. They also provided people with work and clothes. Professional people, especially doctors, also played a prominent role in the provision of charity. A relief committee was established in Skibberrean and the surrounding districts, and is recognized as saving many lives in the local community. All the Churches in Ireland were very active in the relief efforts, providing various forms of charity and material assistance. The Church of Ireland provided many soup kitchens, but there were accusations that some of these only gave assistance to those who agreed to convert to Protestantism. One group that was particularly active was the Quaker Community. Ireland's small Quaker community provided a large amount of relief, many praised their efforts, and they saved countless of lives.[32]

Large sums of money were donated by members of the Irish community abroad, especially from America. The Irish Diaspora provided a great deal of assistance, and even purchased shiploads of food. Money was donated from across the British Empire and beyond. The Pope and Queen Victoria donated £2,000 each. The Sultan in the Ottoman Empire provided a significant sum of money, as well. Many non-religious charities were also very active. The British Relief Association was one such group. Established by Lionel de Rothschild and other wealthy business people and nobles, it raised money throughout England, America, Europe, and Australia. The Association's funding drive greatly benefited from a letter from Queen Victoria appealing for money in order to relieve the distress in Ireland.[33] In total, the Relief Association raised tens of millions in today's money and helped to alleviate the distress of thousands. The Choctaw Nation in Oklahoma provided significant donations to Irish Famine relief, having suffered the bitter experience of starvation themselves. Even today, all those who provided assistance to Ireland during its darkest hour are still fondly remembered by the Irish.

[32] Foster, p. 234
[33] Cork Examiner, January 8th 1847.

The British government introduced a series of local dispensaries throughout Ireland. Nearly every locality had a doctor and some medical staff who provided medical treatment at the dispensaries. Many of these doctors were gifted, and provided free treatment to the poor and the starving. The Catholic and Protestant Churches ran hospitals which provided free health care to many victims of the Famine and saved many lives. Many Irish doctors and nurses gave freely gave their service to the poor during the Famine. Many gave their lives when they died from infectious diseases they contracted as a result of tending the sick. Despite this, the Irish health system was overwhelmed. There were simply too many sick and starving people to help, medical science at the time was too basic to make a serious difference, and many hundreds of thousands of people died from diseases that are easily treatable today.

As noted above, Irish society was dominated both politically and economically by large landowners, many of whom were peers or members of the landed nobility. A large number of landlords were absentee landlords who left the management of their vast estates and rent collection to agents, many of whom were Catholics. Many landlords were indifferent to the fate of their tenants and did not help them in any way. They demanded their usual level of rent, which were often high, and if they failed to pay, they were evicted, and by 1850, there had been approximately 100,000 who had been evicted. Many of them saw the Famine as an opportunity to clear their land of tenants and use it for commercial farming. In the post famine period, landlords came under extreme pressure to carry the financial burden of relief. The 1849 Encumbered Estate Acts allowed them to have more financial freedom. After clearing their lands of tenants, some landlords turned their estates into ranches where they breed cattle, which they then sold to Britain for a high price. Not all landlords were willing to exploit their tenants, however. To the contrary, there were many cases where landlords helped their tenants, providing them with food and/or reduced rent. There were even cases where landlords went bankrupt as a result of their efforts to help distressed tenants. Overall, the reaction of the majority of Irish landlords was uncaring and unhelpful. Many in the British government were unhappy with the response of the landlords. This is evident if we compare the situation in Ireland to that of Scotland. The Scottish Highlands were very similar to Ireland, and in the late 1840s, the local potato crop failed,[34] however, the Scottish landlords, unlike the Irish landlords, helped their tenants, and there was no great loss of life in the Highlands as a result.

The British government in London was responsible for the organising of assistance to the starving Irish. The government was initially informed of the problems with the potato crop in 1844. Their first response was to strengthen existing laws with respect to public order. The authorities in London believed that famine could lead to civil unrest or outright rebellion. Many Irish historians believed that the British government under the able Sir Robert Peel initially did all that was reasonable, given the existing conditions. Peel had served in the Irish administration in the 1830s, and was very familiar with conditions in the country. His administration purchased

---

[34] Woodham-Smith, Cecil (1991) [1962], The Great Hunger: Ireland 1845–1849, Penguin

large quantities of maize from North America to feed the Irish poor. Initially, Irish mills could not ground the maize into kernels, and they were useless. The maize was also too hard to eat, and became popularly known as 'Peel's brimstones.' However, after an initial period of time, the supply of maize did help to feed many people when they were given the maize or 'yellow meal' at relief centers. Peel also instituted a series of public work schemes around the country, in which people were given food in return for working on public works projects. Many of these public works were poorly managed, as we have seen, and did not provide much relief as a result, but in many instances they helped local communities and provided much needed food, and often some money. After Peel's failure to repeal the Corn Laws, he resigned, and a new Liberal government under Lord John Russell was formed. This government was far less willing to become involved in Irish affairs on ideological ground. The new Russell administration was influenced by laissez-faire economic theories, and believed that the market could provide a solution to the crisis.[35] Russell was particularly concerned with the idea that the Irish could become dependent on relief and stop working. This led his government to cut back on the amount of food relief they obtained for Ireland, and also led them to cut back on the number of public works, which meant that many people were left without food, work, or money at a particularly difficult time. Just as the Russell government was seeking to reduce relief programs, the situation worsened. In 1847, the potato blight was particularly bad, and much of the crop was lost. However, as the death rate rose, the British government was forced to become more active. The Russell government introduced outdoor relief in the form of soup kitchens and the provision of free food. They also expanded the number of people who were able to receive help in the Workhouses. However, any person who had as little as a quarter of an acre of land were not entitled to any help. Russell's policies were largely seen as having failed when it came to helping the starving Irish. This caused much bitterness at that time, and since.

Since the first reports of the crisis in the Irish food supply, the British government lived in fear of a popular revolt or a nationalist uprising. Ireland was a very unstable society in the period before the Famine, and many secret societies fought a violent campaign against landlords and those they believed were oppressing the people, such as land agents. The British government gave the police and military in Ireland sweeping powers to deal with the unrest. Irish secret societies continued to be active during the Famine, and carried out arson attacks on landlords' properties and the maiming of their cattle. However, the violence was nothing like the level expected. This has perplexed historians and even the authorities at the time, who expected widespread violence from the starving populace, but it seems that the people were too weak and bewildered, and the majority of people had accepted their fate.

There was, however, a minority of people, who believed the Famine was an unprecedented opportunity for Ireland. A group of Catholic intellectuals and journalists formed a revolutionary organisation, called Young Ireland, a nationalist organisation seeking full independence for

---

[35] O Grada, p. 111

Ireland from Britain. The organisation was modelled on similar nationalist organisations in other countries such as Italy. In 1848, there was a wave of revolutions across Europe and many governments fell. The Young Irelanders, inspired by the turn of events, decided to launch a rebellion in Ireland with the goal of complete independence. The leaders of the rebellion believed the revolution could be bloodless, and would therefore be very popular among the masses. The leaders of the rebellion began to travel throughout Leinster and Munster, raising the Flag of Rebellion, seeking to incite the Irish poor and tenant farmers to attack the local police and disobey the government. The police acted quickly, and arrested many thousands, and the rebellion began to fail. The Irish people had suffered too much, and whatever their sympathies, they simply did not have the energy to resist the government and support the rebels. After a violent confrontation in County Tipperary, the rebels dispersed. The leaders of the rebellion were imprisoned, and Young Ireland's leadership were transported to Australia and Bermuda. After the Famine, the Young Irelanders, despite their failure, had greatly influenced nationalist opinion in Ireland.

Chapter 6: The Consequences of the Famine

Before the Famine, the population of Ireland was in the range of eight to eight and a half million. By 1850 it was estimated that the population of Ireland had dropped to six million, or even less. However, the exact number of deaths may never be known, as the majority of those who died were Catholics, and their births and deaths went unrecorded by local authorities. The estimates for the death toll varies, but the lowest figures are three-quarters of a million to one and a half million, generally peaking the accepted estimate, for the number of deaths from the Famine is in the range of 900,000 to one million.[36]

The Famine also caused the birth rate to collapse, as starving women became too weak to have children. This, together with emigration, meant that Ireland witnessed an unprecedented demographic collapse, which continued in the decades after the Famine. According to government figures from 1890, the population of Limerick had decreased remarkably: in 1840 it was 330,000; in 1851, 262,000; and by 1891 there were only 159,000 people in the city and county.

Perhaps the greatest economic impact of the Famine was a change in the nature of landholding and agriculture. Prior to the catastrophe, the vast majority of Irish families lived and worked on farms that were less than two acres in size. They survived on what they could grow, which was mostly potatoes. However, after the Famine, this was no longer possible, and one of the main impacts of the Famine was that farms became larger in order to ensure they were able to provide families with a sustainable level of income. Many landowners, who mostly lived in London or Dublin, sought to exploit the situation in the aftermath of the Famine. Many of their poor tenants

---

[36] Vaughan, W.E; Fitzpatrick, A.J (1978), W. E. Vaughan; A. J. Fitzpatrick, eds., Irish Historical Statistics, Population, 1821/1971, Royal Irish Academy

had left the land and their farms, and the landowners sought to encourage livestock rearing on their estates, which was more profitable. Increasingly, Ireland moved from arable farming to livestock rearing, and many of the landlords who had once rented land to tenant farmers, now became ranches with large numbers of cattle. However, this led to a great deal of unemployment in the country.[37] Many landlords became bankrupt during the Famine, and the overall number of landlords declined as a result, however, those that did remain owned even larger estates. With the decline of landlord ownership came the decline of domestic servants, evidenced by the censuses of 1881 and 1901. In 1881, the total number of servants recorded was over 250,000, or 10 per cent of the working population. In 1901, this had decreased to 135,000 servants, representing 7.5 percent of the working population. The net effect of the Famine was that a small minority of farmers and landlords increased their landholdings, while the majority of the population remained mired in poverty, with little to no economic opportunities. Poverty remained endemic in Irish life. It remained one of the poorest countries in Europe and was fortunate to avoid another, major famine in 1881, in what became known as the 'Little Famine.'

Prior to the Famine, many small farms were sub-divided after the death of the leaseholder. However, after the Great Hunger, this was no longer the case. Increasingly, the eldest son, inherited the land, and his younger siblings either worked the farm or emigrated. The average sizes of farms increased, and many ordinary farmers moved from arable farming to livestock rearing. As a result, the rural economy became increasingly reliant on livestock and dairy farming, and this has remained the case until today. This, in turn, led to a dramatic change in the social structure of the country. The numbers of agricultural laborers declined by 20 percent between 1841 and 1851, while the population of farmers increased from forty to sixty percent between the years of 1841 and 1881.[38] Laborers, cottiers, and small farmers were in decline during the post-famine years, often working as casual wage workers for farmers, and a new middle-class farmer was emerging, who were to dominate Irish society and politics until the late twentieth century.[39][40][41]

The Famine led to great social changes. Prior to the famine, Irish people married young and had large families. This changed because of the end of the practice of subdividing farms. After the horrors of the Famine, Irish people married later in life, and if they did not have a reasonable sized farm or a chance of steady employment, they may not have married at all. It was increasingly common for many family members to stay on family farms as unpaid laborers and

---

[37] The conditions in rural Ireland improved somewhat, as seen in the reduction of the number of one room cabins, but it remained very poor. See Royal Commission into the Condition of the Poorer Classes in Ireland [35], H.C. 1836 xxx, 35.
[38] Virginia Crossman, '*Politics, pauperism and power in late nineteenth-century Ireland,*' (Manchester University Press, 2006) p 146.
[39] Feely (2004), p 39.
[40] Alice Mauger, 'Confinement of the Higher Orders': The Social Role of Private Lunatic Asylums in Ireland, c. 1820-1860,' *Journal for the History of Medicine and Allied Sciences* 67, no. 2 (2012): pp. 281-317
[41] Éamon Ó Cuív, *An Gorta Mór – The impact and legacy of the Great Irish Famine*, Lecture delivered at St. Michael's College, University of Toronto, Canada, (2009).

never marry. As a result of these changes, Ireland had a high rate of single, unmarried people, and this led to social problems. In 1871, 40 per cent of women aged 15 to 45 were married; by 1911, this had fallen to 39 per cent.[42] Alcoholism was a major problem in Ireland, and the country was to eventually experience one of the highest levels of alcoholism in the world. Another major problem in Ireland was mental illness. As a result of poverty, continuing tensions over land and alcoholism meant that the country had very high levels of mental illness. Many were committed to local asylums or to Workhouses.

There was also a big impact on the religious character of Ireland. The majority of the population in Ireland were Catholics (75%), with a large Protestant minority (25%). Ireland was traditionally a very religious society. After the Famine, Irish society became even more religious. Some scholars have suggested that the trauma of the Famine resulted in the people turning to religion for support and hope. In the decades after the Famine, Irish Catholics became renowned for the strict observance of their religion. Prior to the Famine, the Church had been influential, but after the famine, it became all-pervasive. In the decades before the Great Hunger, many cottiers and laborers had mixed Catholicism with ideas from folk religion. The growing power of the Catholic Church meant that people were increasingly orthodox, and many aspects of the traditional Irish culture went into decline, such as the belief in the Banshee.[43] Every year, thousands of Irish people became priests and nuns, or joined religious orders. The Catholic clergy became very powerful in Irish life and society. In the years after the Famine, the Catholic population's strict interpretation of their religion and the growing influence of the Catholic hierarchy worried many in Irish Protestants. This ultimately led to increasing tensions between Catholics and Protestants, which ultimately led to conflict between the two communities throughout the twentieth century.

On the face of it, the Famine led to no real dramatic changes in the political landscape. By 1860, the landlords still controlled the land and much of the wealth of the country, and the British administration in Dublin Castle was as entrenched as ever, though there was a real change in Irish public opinion. Prior to the Famine, the Irish Catholic majority had been happy merely to seek freedom for their religion, and to improve their political and social status, however, the Famine caused much bitterness among the survivors, and in the Irish communities abroad. This fostered the crowd of nationalism. In 1848, the Young Irelanders failed to mobilize the Irish population to end British rule. However, in the decades after the Great Hunger, a significant proportion of the population became increasingly nationalistic, and even began to embrace extremist ideas. For many Irish people, the Famine had poisoned relations with Britain forever, and they wanted complete independence. By the 1860s, there was another attempted nationalist revolution, this time by the Finnian movement, who were inspired by the Young Irelanders. This

---

[42] Maria Luddy, '*Women in Ireland 1800-1918,*' (Cork University Press 1995) p 5.

[43] The Banshee was a spirit who foretold the death of people. See Foster, p. 234.

revolt was also largely unsuccessful. Soon after its failure, the Irish Revolutionary Brotherhood was born, which, in turn, led to the formation of the Irish Republican Army. The impact of the Famine was that it left a residue of bitterness against Britain, which led to extreme nationalism to become entrenched in Irish political life. To this day, there are still violent nationalist groups active in Ireland.

As noted above, the impact of the Famine varied from region to region, and it had a marked impact on the ethnic background of Ireland itself. The famine hit the west and the south of the island the hardest. These areas were largely Gaelic or Irish speaking. In the west in particular, the majority of people spoke Irish, as their forefathers had done. They also had a distinctive Irish culture, markedly different from other areas of the country. However, Irish had been in decline since the eighteenth century, and people were increasingly adopting English as their first language, as well as their modern customs, which had a devastating impact on the Irish language and culture. The strongholds of Gaelic culture and language were disproportionately impacted by the Great Hunger and the subsequent high levels of emigration. Many Gaelic speakers died as a result of the Famine, or they emigrated abroad. The numbers of Irish speakers were much reduced as a result, and by 1900, there were only a few Gaelic enclaves in the west and south and on remote islands. The Irish government has tried to revive the language, but it is on the brink of extinction, counting the Gaelic language as another victim of the Famine.

The Famine and the British government's handling of the crisis left much bitterness in Ireland and served to radicalize many. Some have argued that the British government, allied with the Anglo-Irish landowners, sought to deliberately starve the Irish Catholic population to make sure that they did not challenge British rule, and to allow the landlords to clear the land of tenants so they could pursue the more lucrative pastoral farming. Many have argued that this amounted to genocide, that it was a deliberate policy of exterminating a nation or group, in this case, the Irish Catholics. In 1996, an American historical study argued that the Irish Famine had, indeed, amounted to a genocide. The British government deliberately failed to respond in an adept way to the Famine, and to provide proper relief as part of a policy of extermination. In this regard, the Irish famine (1945-1850) could be seen as akin to the Soviet-made Famine in the Ukraine in the 1930s. There are precedents for this in Irish history, in the use of Famine, to secure political objectives. During the Tudor conquest of Ireland in the late sixteenth century, famine was used to conquer the island, which resulted in the loss of half of the population. The majority of Irish historians are against this view, and many extreme nationalists (no lovers of the British) do not claim that the Famine was a deliberate attempt to exterminate the Irish, disagreeing that the famine was an attempt at genocide. The British government's response was not adequate. Certainly there were many in London who were not sympathetic to the Irish. In general, the British did a lot to help the Irish, and their relief programmes did save many lives. There is a widespread agreement that the British relief effort was not satisfactory, and that more could have been done, but given the times and the level of technology available to the British, their relief efforts would have been limited, anyway. In general, there is a widespread agreement that the

British failed to manage the Famine properly and that they neglected the Irish in their hour of need, but this does not amount to deliberate and intentional genocide.

Either way, the Famine was undoubtedly a tragedy for Ireland. It changed the island forever and led to mass starvation and an unprecedented humanitarian crisis, resulting in the deaths of approximately a million people. It decisively shaped Irish society for many decades, and its effects are still felt, even to the present day. The country in the aftermath of the Great Famine became increasingly dominated by large farmers, its economy based on the rearing and breeding of cattle. The Famine resulted in increased tensions between Catholics and Protestants. The Famine and its after effects had a profound impact on the Irish psyche, resulting in the population becoming increasingly religious. The Catholic Church, already powerful in the country, became the dominant social and cultural institution on the island of Ireland, and it remained so until the late twentieth century. For many decades after Irish independence, the Republic of Ireland was widely viewed as a Catholic theocracy.

The disaster also dealt a death blow to the Gaelic language and culture. While the Famine had an impact on some areas more than others, it caused great suffering among all people on the island of Ireland. The Famine's most durable legacy was the continuing high levels of emigration from the country, which lasted until at least the 1960s. This was a tragedy for Ireland, and as a result of emigration, the Irish population has still not bounced back to its pre-famine level. The catastrophe also damaged Anglo-Irish relations, arguably until the present day. This led to the development of many extremist nationalist groups in Ireland, and as a result, political violence became endemic in Irish society throughout much of the twentieth century.

In addition, the Famine led to mass emigration from the country, which was to have significant consequences for many nations, especially in North America. Irish emigrants helped countries such as Canada and America to fulfil their potential and become great countries.

Due to all of these effects, the Irish Famine was truly an event of global significance.

Felix O's picture of a memorial to victims

A mural in Belfast about the Famine

Alan MC's picture of a memorial in Dublin

Online Resources

Other 19th century history titles by Charles River Editors

Other titles about the Potato Famine on Amazon

Bibliography

Donnelly, James S (2005), *The Great Irish Potato Famine*, Sutton Publishing.

Gray, Peter (1995), *The Irish Famine*, New York: Harry N. Abrams, Inc.

Hayden, Tom (1998), Hayden, Tom; O'Connor, Garrett; Harty, Patricia, eds., *Irish hunger: personal reflections on the legacy of the famine*, Roberts Rinehart Publishers.

Laxton, Edward (1997), *The Famine Ships: The Irish Exodus to America 1846–51*, Bloomsbury.

Litton, Helen (1994), *The Irish Famine: An Illustrated History*, Wolfhound Press.

Ó Gráda, Cormac (1993), *Ireland before and after the Famine: Explorations in Economic History 1800–1925*, Manchester University Press.

Ó Gráda, Cormac (2000), *Black '47 and Beyond: The Great Irish Famine in History, Economy, and Memory*, Princeton University Press.

Ó Gráda, Cormac (2006), *Ireland's Great Famine: Interdisciplinary Perspectives*, Dublin Press.

Póirtéir, Cathal (1995), *The Great Irish Famine*, RTÉ/Mercier Press.

Made in the USA
Columbia, SC
20 February 2019